Happy Mail

Keep in touch with cool & stylish
handmade snail mail!

EUNICE & SABRINA MOYLE
PHOTOGRAPHS BY ALEX BRONSTAD

Brimming with creative inspiration, how-to projects, and useful information to enrich your everyday life, Quarto Knows is a favorite destination for those pursuing their interests and passions. Visit our site and dig deeper with our books into your area of interest: Quarto Creates, Quarto Cooks, Quarto Homes, Quarto Lives, Quarto Drives, Quarto Explores, Quarto Gifts, or Quarto Kids.

© 2017 Quarto Publishing Group USA Inc.
Artwork © Hello!Lucky, LLC

First Published in 2017 by Walter Foster Jr., an imprint of The Quarto Group.
6 Orchard Road, Suite 100, Lake Forest, CA 92630, USA.
T (949) 380-7510 **F** (949) 380-7575 **www.QuartoKnows.com**

Walter Foster Jr. titles are also available at discount for retail, wholesale, promotional, and bulk purchase. For details, contact the Special Sales Manager by email at specialsales@quarto.com or by mail at The Quarto Group, Attn: Special Sales Manager, 401 Second Avenue North, Suite 310, Minneapolis, MN 55401 USA.

ISBN: 978-1-63322-367-7

Printed in China
10 9 8 7 6 5 4 3 2

TABLE OF CONTENTS

4

Introduction

You probably know how awesome it feels to receive a handmade letter or card by good old snail mail or hand delivery. You probably also know how satisfying it is to watch your creativity flow onto a blank piece of paper and unfold into something brand new. But if you feel a little unsure about your ability to draw, or if you don't considered yourself an artist, you might also struggle with creating your own handmade letters and cards.

We wrote this book to help you! Try out some of our fun, fabulous projects, and you will master hand-lettering and doodling in no time. If you can draw a smiley face and write your name, you can make your own awesome hand-lettered designs. Truth is, you've been doing it since you were a little kid!

So take this book as your invitation to settle in and start getting creative. Handmade and handwritten correspondence is truly awesome—you never know where it will lead. It can inspire fun conversations, make someone's day, and even spark new ideas, new connections, and new friendships.

SO GO AHEAD AND GET STARTED AND HAVE TONS OF FUN ALONG THE WAY!

LETTER WRITING TOOLS

There are lots of great writing and drawing tools out there, but over time, we've discovered that this group of tried-and-true workhorses make projects come out great every time.

Card Stock Card stock is the ideal canvas for handmade cards. We love 80- to 100-lb. white card stock, which you can buy in pads or reams. Anything heavier than 100 lb. will make your card difficult to fold. Equally, text-weight paper is too flimsy and won't absorb ink or paint well—plus it tends to buckle. We also love multi-media and hot-press watercolor paper for their absorbency (essential for painted projects!) and texture.

Envelopes We love plain white envelopes with a deep "V" flap because you can design your own cool envelope liners or decorate the envelope itself. For most of our projects, we've used Paper Source Luxe White envelopes, which have a nice thick texture and easily absorb ink and paint. If you're inclined to use colored envelopes, Paper Source also has our favorite selection of colors and shapes. For the projects in this book, we've chosen A7 envelopes (which measure $5\frac{1}{4}$" x $7\frac{1}{4}$"). Always makes sure your card is $\frac{1}{4}$ inch smaller than the envelope so it glides in and out smoothly. You can buy envelopes in bulk from your local art-supply store or online.

Pencils In most of our projects, we use pencils for light tracing before we ink or color; any standard pencil will do. (We love old-fashioned yellow school pencils!) A moderately hard pencil can be more forgiving than a softer one since it's easier to erase later (we like HB or B). We encourage you to be intentionally loose when sketching your design. Hold your pencil with a relaxed grip and make quick gestural lines, focusing on getting the general idea and layout down. Don't sweat the details; you can fill those in later. Plus, you can always erase! Since these are easy and quick projects, don't be afraid to try each one a few times— you'll learn something new each time, and you'll be able to refine your approach to make it your own.

Erasers Having an eraser on hand makes it easy to erase pencil marks from your initial sketching. We personally like a white plastic eraser, such as Staedtler Mars, but any eraser will do—even the one on the back of your pencil!

Brush-Tip Pen Brush-tip pens give an artful, loose feel to anything you write. Their tapered tips, which look just like the tip of a paintbrush, allow you to change the width of your stroke as you write simply by changing the angle and the amount of applied pressure. Different stroke thicknesses on the down-strokes and cross-strokes help achieve distinctive looks—which is the secret to great hand-lettering! Our favorite brush-tip pen is the Tombow® pen, but feel free to experiment with other calligraphy or paint pens.

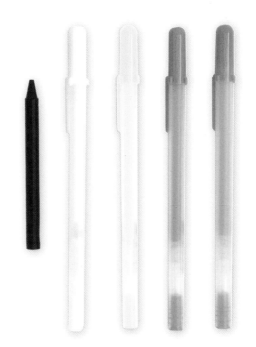

Felt-Tip Pens Black felt-tip pens are great for illustration line work. The felt-tip gives the line an artistic pen-and-ink quality that lends itself to hand illustration. We love the Pilot Fineliner, the Stylist, or a fine-tip Sharpie®. Feel free to experiment with colored pens too!

Black Crayon A simple black crayon is a fantastic tool for making line work that has personality and texture. Crayon is easy to draw with, and it gives off a playful vibe. It reminds us of the carefree days when we were little and spent tons of time drawing with nothing but some plain paper and crayons.

Gel Pens Gel pens are opaque and fun to draw with. They come in all kinds of awesome colors and textures—Shimmer! Glitter! Pearlescent! Neon! We're partial to Sakura Gelly Rolls® for their vibrant neons and opaque whites, which make art on a dark surface pop out. Get yourself a few, and start exploring. You'll be so glad you did!

LETTER WRITING BASICS

Writing a letter is simple, but also profound. The best letters go beyond small talk: They are a way to express your best self and authentically connect with others. A letter should never feel like you were forced to write it. Instead, it should feel spontaneous and true to you. So don't censor yourself or worry about making a good impression. Just be you and watch what unfolds!

You can play with the format of your card or letter (feel free to get creative!), but note that it should contain the following elements:

❶ Date Not essential, but it can be nice to write the date in the upper-right corner of your letter. That way, when you and your friend are old and gray and looking back at your letters while sipping prune juice, you'll remember what era it was from!

❷ Opening Salutation Greeting your friend by name is the first step to starting a letter conversation and making a personal connection. People love to see their names in writing! Your salutation can be the traditional "Dear Abby," but if that feels too formal, you can use "Hey, Jude!", "Hiya, Jo!", "Hello there, friend!", "Hola!", or simply "Alex." Feel free to get creative.

❸ Body This is where you write! Your card or letter can be a simple conversational catch-up recounting recent events or things that are on your mind. You can also incorporate a pun or funny message (like a lot of the projects in this book!), a quote, a memory, a description of something that happened to you that reminded you of your friend, something that you read or watched, a list, or even a poem. The key thing is to keep the recipient in mind when you're writing—write something personal. If you're writing a longer letter, organize your thoughts by topic, and start a new paragraph when switching subjects.

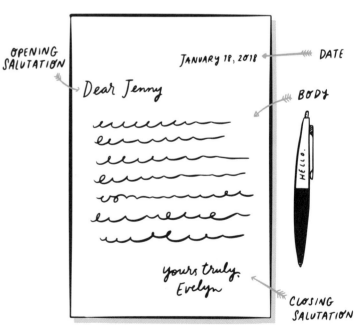

4 Closing Salutation This is where you sign off. Traditional closings include "Sincerely," "Love," and "Yours Truly," but we love to use more casual closings like "XOXO," "'Til Soon," or "Ciao!" You could also come up with a funny phrase or an inside joke. Think of an adjective, value, or phrase that connects you and your friend. Try "In solidarity," "United in silliness," "Strength and honor," "With style and, sometimes, substance," "Yours in good times and heinous ones," "Yours in outrage and optimism," or "Your official co-founder, Glass Half Full Club." The sillier the better—it's always great to end a letter with a laugh!

Here are a couple sample letters to get your idea generator firing:

SAMPLE "JUST BECAUSE" LETTER

Dear Anne,

Just a quick note to say you're awesome, and I'm so glad you're my friend! You've always got my back, and you're such an amazing listener! Thanks for being the GOAT.

xoxo Jane

PRO TIP Make your "just because" short but artistic—use your creative hand-lettering skills to fill the whole page!

SAMPLE THANK YOU LETTER

Dear Amy,

Thank you so much for the amazing bracelet you gave me for my birthday! It is so pretty—I've been wearing it every day. Seriously! It reminds me of our friendship and of you—beautiful, sparkly, and goes with everything! Thanks for being such a thoughtful, funny, fierce friend.

Your "accessory" in love + friendship,

Sarah

HOW TO MAIL YOUR LETTER

Once you've created your card or letter, you need to make sure it gets there in one piece! This is not as simple as just hitting "send." But that's the beauty of good old snail mail—whoever gets it knows that sending it took real effort!

Here are some tips to make sure the post office gets your letter to the right place.

Addressing your Envelope
First, you'll need your recipient's address. Feel free to ping them on social media to ask for it, and once you have it, stash it someplace safe so you don't need to bug them again!

Recipient Address
Address the envelope to the recipient in the front-center area of the envelope, like so:

Full Name (e.g. Sarah Adams)
Street Address (e.g. 100 Main Street)
Apartment or Unit # if applicable (e.g. Apartment 5F)
City, State Zip Code (e.g. Springfield, Illinois 62701)
Country (if mailing overseas)

Write legibly, and make sure the address stays $1/4$ inch from the bottom edge of the envelope. The post office puts bar code labels on the bottom edge for mail-sorting purposes, so anything written in that zone might get covered up by the label. This could cause your mail to get lost.

Return Address
Write your own address either in the upper-left corner of the front of the envelope, or on the flap. This allows the post office to send it back to you in the event that you misaddress your envelope.

Stamp
Put a stamp in the top-right corner of your envelope. The best bet is a "Forever" stamp since the value will always be correct, even if the price of stamps changes. The "Forever" will be enough postage for a typical folded card (single sheet of card stock) or a few sheets of text-weight letter paper.

PRO TIP
Square envelopes and envelopes containing rigid objects cost more to mail. Use the postage calculator on www.usps.com to find the correct amount of postage.

RETURN ADDRESS

Evelyn Wood
5490 Linwood Cr
Excelsior, MN 55331

AIRMAIL
FEB 2
9 PM
AIRMAIL

POSTAGE PAID

JENNY STATLER
3 Highland Ave.
San Francisco CA.
9 4 1 1 8

ADDRESS

If your card is made of bulkier stuff, though, consider weighing it or adding on some extra postage just to be safe. Always check international postage rates before sending mail overseas. (You can look up the correct postage rates on www.usps.com.)

Stuff, Seal, and Send

Once your envelope is addressed and stamped, put your card in so that it faces the recipient right-side up when pulled out. Then lick the envelope flap, and press down firmly to give it a good seal. If you're worried about the envelope popping open (or have a lot of envelopes to lick!), you can always use a glue stick. Finally, drop your letter in your nearest post box or at the post office, or leave it in your mailbox for your postal carrier to pick up (if you have an old-fashioned mail box, put the little red flag up to signal that you've got outgoing mail!).

Once mailed, your letter should take anywhere from a couple of days to a week to arrive. Enjoy the days, or even weeks, of zen that pass as you await a reply. Even if you don't get a response, you've put something good out in the world! Enjoy the journey, and savor some slow communication!

GET READY TO WRITE

Creating a handmade card or letter takes precious time which, if you're like us, might feel in short supply. That's why slowing down and putting pen to paper is such a fabulous gift to yourself! Making space to create leads to a state of bliss and promotes creative flow. When we write, we're creating and connecting rather than reacting and deciding. It's such a happy feeling!

Before diving into a project, we like to set up our physical workspace. Clear off a desk or table, and lay out your letter-writing supplies. Put away any distractions, like your phone or laptop, and turn on some inspiring music (or work in peace and quiet). We love creating in a space that has natural light, so if that's available to you, set yourself up there. You can even go outdoors if the weather is nice!

Next, we like to get into the right headspace for creative genius. Check in with yourself. How are you feeling? Is there anything you need to clear from your mind to be fully engaged in creating? If so, take a few deep breaths, and breathe away any distracting thoughts.

Next, think about the person you are going to write to. Where are they right now? What is going on in their life? How might they be feeling? What might they need to hear from you? How can you make their life better through your connection? Take a second to reflect on the big picture of your relationship. What do you most adore or appreciate about them? What makes them unique? Why are they in your life? What drew you together, and what keeps you connected? Whatever it is, there is a reason why you are friends; use it as inspiration to write!

Next, think about your reason for writing. Are you writing to say thank you, congrats, or happy birthday? Are you writing to reconnect or offer support? Is there a silly story you can tell or a fond memory you can share? Do you have big news that you're dying to break, or do you want to shout-out appreciation or encouragement? What you write doesn't matter as much as the feelings behind your words; just start from a place of good vibes and let the words flow freely.

And finally, remember: The absence of a backspace and spellcheck are key parts of the beauty and authenticity of a handwritten note. (If you want, write a draft of your letter before setting it in ink; this can help with planning how much space you'll need to fit your words on your card and will make minor revisions easier.) This is your chance to conquer your fears, one handwritten letter at a time!

WRITING PROMPTS

Sometimes we just need a little nudge to get the words flowing. Here are a few of our favorite prompts for some of the most common letter-writing occasions.

Thank You

Thank you so much for the thoughtful gift! I can't believe you remembered that I love ____. I'll use it the next time I...

Wow, you made my day! Thank you so much for...

Thank you so much for helping me with ____. You are an amazing friend! So grateful!

Love

Words can't express how awesome you are, but here's my best try...

You make me so happy! Here's just a few reasons why...

You're the best ____ I could ever wish for! Who else would...

Apologies

I'm sorry I ____. It was wrong because ____. In the future, I'll ____. Will you please forgive me? (Add some humor if it feels appropriate!)

I messed up. Will you forgive me?

So grateful for your friendship, and promise to be more thoughtful in the future!

Forgiveness

I forgive you for ____, and I'm sorry I messed up too! All good! Let's be friends!

Don't worry about what happened. I forgive you... but only if you promise to forgive me the next time I ____. (Insert something really silly here!)

Mother's Day / Father's Day

Thanks for being such a rock star mom / dad. Here are a few of the ways I think you're stellar...

Birthday

Happy birthday to the most ____ person I know!

Top wishes for you on your birthday...

REASONS TO WRITE A LETTER

Not quite convinced of the rewards of writing a hand-lettered card instead of sending another text, email, or IM? Here's a list of reasons to dive in. Invite your friends to join you!

- A letter is personal, private, and permanent.

- Writing thoughts and feelings down in a letter makes them known and real.

- Letter-writing takes time, and the process helps us appreciate the people we love.

- A letter is a shared object and a shared experience that helps our friendships grow deeper.

- Handwriting is more personal than typewritten text.

- Handwriting helps us generate creative thoughts and ideas.

- Letters give us a reason to be creative and expressive.

- Letters can be very diverse—they can include words, pictures, quotes, lists, poems, questions, and more.

- Letters help us stay connected to people who don't often use computers.

- Handwritten letters are rare, which makes them special to receive.

- Letter-writing is a form of contemplation that helps us get to know ourselves better.

- Writing a letter helps us develop our voices.

- Letters give us a reason to express gratitude, which is scientifically linked to happiness.

- Letters let us say things that would be hard to say in person or on social media.

- A letter is a more meaningful gift than most material things.

- Letters are 1-to-1 instead of 1-to-many.

- Letters re-humanize relationships.

30 LETTERS IN 30 DAYS CHALLENGE

A few years ago, thanks to our friend Tess Darrow at Egg Press, we started co-hosting a 30-day letter-writing challenge each April—National Card and Letter Writing Month—which we called Write_On. We started by inviting a handful of friends to join us in writing 30 letters in 30 days. Eventually, over 10,000 people were joining us each April! Below are some of the many reasons to write letters that we came up with. Let them inspire you, or come up with your own!

☐ Write a thank you note to someone you see every day.

☐ Write a letter to your future self.

☐ Write a thank you note to your barista, your bus driver, or someone else whose good work may go unnoticed.

☐ Send a note to someone who bugs you telling them what you appreciate about them.

☐ Send a letter with a fun activity in it.

☐ Send a text (a one-sentence note) through the mail!

☐ Ask a friend things you don't know about them.

☐ Send a letter to a kid you know who's just learning to read or write.

☐ Write a haiku about the recipient.

☐ Send a note to an older person in your life who might not get much mail (or who might not use the computer much).

☐ Write a letter remembering someone who passed away.

☐ Send someone a list of places you'd like to go with them someday.

- [ ] Thank someone for being a great role model.
- [ ] Send a letter in multiple parts—they'll have to wait for the next episode.
- [ ] Write down your favorite quote and give it to a stranger.
- [ ] Include a self-addressed, stamped envelope so you get a letter back too!
- [ ] Write a note to your letter carrier.
- [ ] Draw a self-portrait and send it to your friend.
- [ ] Write a letter to someone you just saw to let them know how nice it was to see them.
- [ ] Send an apology that you have been putting off.
- [ ] Find a small, special thing (a trinket, a photo, a candy) and include it in your letter.
- [ ] Write to a cause you support, encouraging them and telling them how much their actions mean to you.
- [ ] Send fan mail to your favorite celebrity!
- [ ] Write to your mom or dad about how they've inspired you.
- [ ] Let a friend know you've been thinking of them.
- [ ] Mail a birthday card to a Facebook friend—it's OK if it's after their birthday!
- [ ] Write a kind and encouraging note and hand it to the next homeless person you see. (You can even include cash for a warm cup of coffee!)
- [ ] Draw a picture of you and your friend together—the sillier the better!
- [ ] Write to a childhood friend about what you remember about them.
- [ ] Send a letter of solidarity to someone who may be feeling alone.

Lettering Styles

Hand-lettering makes letter-writing fun! Our favorite styles are loose and naïve—they're a breeze to get the hang of and they allow us to be more free with our creativity. We love mixing letter styles and capitalization, and combining bold strokes with thinner connectors. Note: Choosing the right pen for your style makes a huge difference! For bolder styles, a brush-tip pen that allows you to vary the stroke width is essential. For more precise styles, a fine felt-tip marker is best.

Use this next section to practice different hand-lettering styles (we've provided several of our faves for you to try!). Experiment with them, practice and polish your technique, and make them your own! If you're not comfortable lettering directly on your page, here's a trick: Find a font you like on your computer, type up your message, and print it out. Then use a tracing board to trace over your message. (Or tape the printout to a window, place your card over it, and trace.)

PAPER CUT ALPHABET

This style is created with a felt-tip pen. Draw the outlines, and then fill them in.
Remember: Imperfection is cool!

A B C D E F
G H I J K L
M N O P Q R
S T U V W
X Y Z

← DRAW THE SHAPES

FILL IT IN ↓ R

YOUR TURN!

BRUSH LETTERING

This style is created with a Tombow® pen. Try varying the pressure for thick and thin strokes—more pressure equals a thicker stroke, and less pressure equals a thinner stroke.

A B C D
E F G H
I J K L
M N O P
Q R S T
U V W X
Y Z

SIDE OF PEN

POINT OF PEN

Your turn!

OPEN ALPHABET

Draw this alphabet with a fine felt-tip pen. Each part of the letter is drawn as two parallel lines that overlap at the corners.

YOUR TURN!

_____

- -

_____

_____

- -

_____

_____

- -

_____

_____

- -

_____

_____

- -

_____

_____

- -

_____

Ribbon Alphabet

Use a fat marker for this ribbon type, and add the "ribbon ends" afterward with a fine felt-tip pen. Note that cursive lettering really doesn't work in all caps. For lowercase letters, write in cursive, making the letters round and fat. Finish by adding in the ribbon ends and squaring off the parts where the letters might "fold" (like at the top of the p in "alphabet" above).

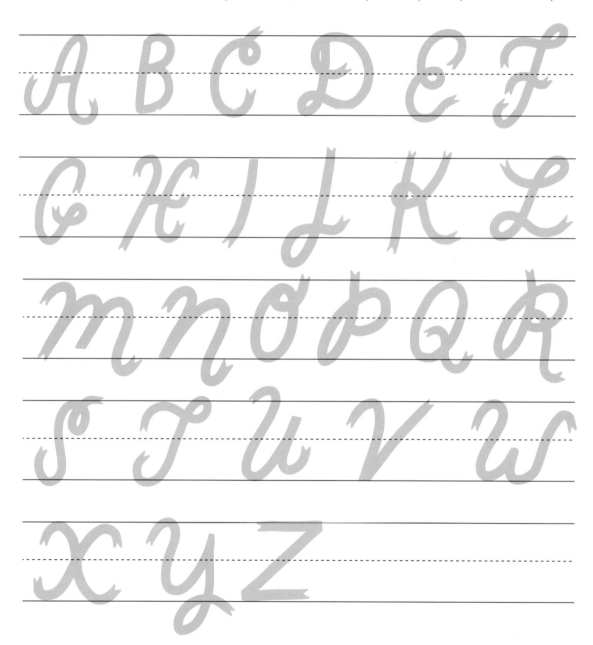

Your turn!

STORYBOOK ALPHABET

This alphabet is drawn with a fine felt-tip pen. Start with the thicker parts of the letter by drawing two parallel lines and filling them in. Finish the letter by adding the thinner parts with single lines, also adding the serifs, or the flair on the ends.

A B C D E F

G H I J K L

M N O P Q R

S T U V W

X Y Z

YOUR TURN!

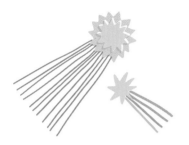

Let's Practice!

_____

- -

_____

_____

- -

_____

_____

- -

_____

_____

- -

_____

_____

- -

_____

LET'S PRACTICE!

Hand-lettering PROJECTS

We love the look of hand-drawn illustrations combined with hand-lettering. Throw in a quirky or funny concept and a punchy, punny greeting, and it gets even better. A more stylishly simple design makes the projects quick and easy to do...oh so satisfying. We love to keep our designs light-hearted and inspired by the latest trends. A little neon never hurts either!

In this next section, you'll find card ideas for a variety of different letter-writing occasions. You can follow the projects to the letter, or just use them as a starting point for developing your own ideas. Have fun making and sending them by mail. We hope they inspire you to discover your own creative voice and that sharing them makes the folks you love super happy!

CUT PAPER Love Notes

This project takes a fun and bold graphic approach.
There's so much room for pattern play with black type overlays!
This one's going on the wall afterward...

MATERIALS

- *8½" x 11" sheet of white card stock*

- *Black paper*

- *Neon pink paper (we used Astrobrights® text weight)*

- *White Gelly Roll® pen*

- *Scissors*

- *Pencil (optional)*

- *Eraser (optional)*

- *Glue stick*

- *Black felt-tip pen*

- *Craft knife*

- *Cutting mat or magazine*

- *Ruler*

- *A7 white envelope*

Additional materials for Eye Heart You! card

- *Neon yellow and white paper*

- *Yellow highlighter*

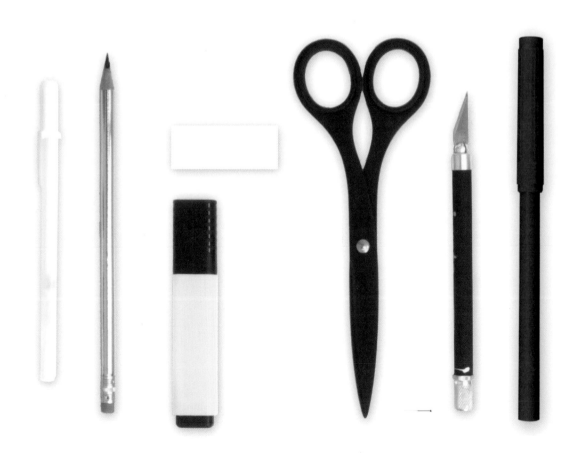

CARD

❶ Make your card. Fold a piece of card stock in half, and using a craft knife, ruler, and cutting mat or magazine, cut the card to 5" x 7," folded.

❷ With scissors, cut out approximately 15 2-inch lip shapes from neon pink paper.

❸ Glue lip shapes to the front of your card to create a pattern, with some going off the edge. Trim those to be flush with the card's edge.

❹ Add lip details with a white Gelly Roll® pen.

❺ Using scissors, cut out the letters. Ours are approximately 1 $\frac{3}{4}$ inches tall. (You can also trace the letters first with a pencil to help guide you.)

❻ Glue the letters to the front of the card. If there are leftover pencil marks, erase them.

For the **Eye Heart You** card, cut the various shapes out of paper, and glue them to the front of your card. For the eye, stack a piece of white and a piece of black paper, and cut out an almond shape. Then trim the white shape down about $\frac{1}{8}$ inch to create the black outline of the eye. Cut a black circle (center of eye) to fit into the black almond shape. Glue skinny black rectangles (lashes) to the card first, and then layer the black almond shape, the white almond shape, and the circle on top.

BISOUS ENVELOPE

❶ Cut out approximately 10 hearts from neon pink paper. Glue them at random to the inside flap of the envelope.

❷ When you get to the glue line of the envelope, lightly mark the place where the heart and the glue line meet with a pencil. Trim off the part that overlaps the glue line, and then glue down the heart, lining up the cut edge with the glue line. Tuck some into the envelope opening so they peep out a bit. This creates the illusion of an envelope liner.

❸ Draw Xs with a black felt-tip pen in between the hearts.

EYE HEART YOU! ENVELOPE

❶ Cut out approximately 4 small hearts from neon pink paper.

❷ Glue them at random to the inside flap of the envelope.

❸ Draw eyes scattered around the hearts, cutting some off at the glue line to create the illusion of an envelope liner.

❹ With a yellow highlighter, add some lightning bolts and dash marks to fill out the pattern.

BISOUS MEANS KISSES IN FRENCH.

Quote Note

We love finding fun, inspiring quotes and illustrating them. Turning quotes into note cards is a great way to share the love. Doodle or hand-letter your own inspirational quote, and give it to a friend or even someone you don't know that well!

MATERIALS

- *8½" x 11" sheet of black card stock*
- *A variety of neon Gelly Roll® pens, including white*
- *Craft knife*
- *Cutting mat or magazine*
- *Ruler*
- *A7 envelope (we used white)*
- *Pencil (optional)*
- *Eraser (optional)*

CARD

1 Make your card. Fold a piece of black card stock in half, and using a craft knife, ruler, and cutting mat or magazine, cut the card to 5" x 7," folded.

2 Draw parallel horizontal lines in the middle of your card with a white Gelly Roll® pen, and write the message on the lines. Feel free to pencil it first if you're not confident in your freehand.

3 Doodle stars and comets around the text. Leave space between colors to make shapes pop.

ENVELOPE

1 Using a variety of neon Gelly Roll® pens, doodle stars and comets all over the envelope.

IDEAS TO TRY

- "When it rains, look for rainbows." (doodle rainbows, raindrops, clouds)

- "A smooth sea never made for a skillful sailor." (doodle waves, sailboats, sea creatures)

- "Be a Froot Loop in a world of Cheerios." (doodle O's)

- "Always be yourself, unless you can be a unicorn. Then always be a unicorn." (doodle unicorn, stars, rainbows)

- "What makes you different is what makes you beautiful." (doodle flowers or stars)

EMOJi Note

Everyone loves a good emoji. Why not make it tangible? Straight from the heart, this card is a modern twist on pop art. Mine your phone for more emoji ideas!

MATERIALS

- *8½" x 11" sheet of white card stock*
- *Emoji templates (see page 95)*
- *Neon pink and Neon yellow paper (we used Astrobrights® text weight)*
- *Black paper*
- *White paper*

- *Brown paper*
- *Black Tombow® Dual Brush Pen*
- *Scissors*
- *Pencil*
- *Eraser*

- *Glue stick*
- *Craft knife*
- *Cutting mat or magazine*
- *Ruler*
- *A7 white envelope*

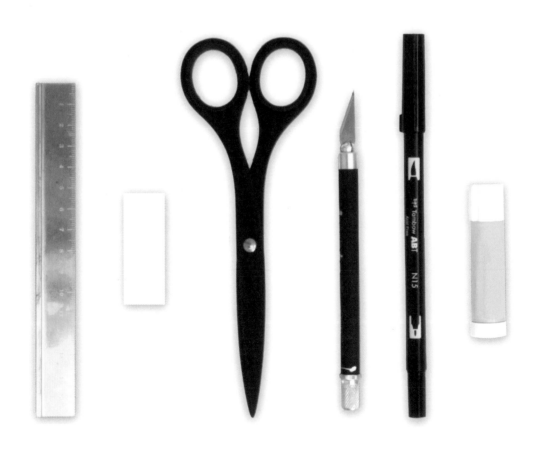

HEART EYES

FOR YOU!

YOU

ARE THE

CARD

1. Make your card. Fold a piece of card stock in half, and using a craft knife, ruler, and cutting mat or magazine, cut the card down to 5″ x 7,″ folded.

2. Using the template, cut out the various shapes from appropriately colored paper.

3. Glue the various cutouts to the front of the card.

4. With a pencil, lightly trace out the placement of the message.

5. Trace the letters with a Tombow® pen, varying pressure and angle to create a cool hand-lettered look.

IDEAS TO TRY

Who says poop has to be brown? We think the shape is pretty iconic, so you can get creative with outside-the-box neon poop if you're feeling inspired!

ENVELOPE

1. Cut out approximately 13 hearts from neon pink paper using the heart from the heart eyes template. The fastest way is to accordion fold a piece of paper and cut out several at a time.

2. Starting in the middle, glue down a row of hearts. When you get to the glue line of the envelope, lightly mark the glue line on the heart with a pencil. Trim off the part that overlaps the glue line, and then glue down the heart, lining up the cut edge with the glue line.

3. Continue with the next row, staggering the hearts so each heart falls between the two below it, until you have covered the entire inside flap of the envelope.

I Love You More than...

Let your creativity run free with this one! Make a list of things you love, and pick your favorite ones to doodle. The recipient will be so flattered to see how much you truly adore them!

MATERIALS

- *8½" x 11" sheet of white card stock*
- *Fine black felt-tip pen (we used a Pilot Fineliner)*
- *Slightly thicker black felt-tip pen (we used a Pentel® Sign Pen)*
- *Neon Gelly Roll® pens*
- *Pencil*
- *Eraser*
- *Craft knife*
- *Cutting mat or magazine*
- *Ruler*
- *A7 white envelope*

CARD

1. Make your card. Fold a piece of card stock in half, and using a craft knife, ruler, and cutting mat or magazine, cut the card to 5" x 7," folded.

2. Write your message with the thicker black pen, and doodle a pattern of things you love around it with the fine-tip pen. Draw only the outlines of the illustrations; add the details later so they don't muddy when you add the color.

3. Color in the illustrations with Gelly Roll® pens, adding extra flourishes like stars, dotted lines, and rainbows, and then add final details with the fine-tip pen.

ENVELOPE

1. Draw a pattern of rainbows with Gelly Roll® pens, cutting off the pattern along the glue line of the envelope to create the illusion of an envelope liner.

PRO TIP

Lightly sketch your message and doodles with a pencil first to avoid mistakes.

List Letter

We love making lists. Tell your bestie what you like most about him/her, and don't be confined to the size of the card—let your love run free! Don't forget to customize the portrait to resemble the recipient.

- *Sheet of lightweight paper large enough to be cut down to 10" x 14" (we used light blue)*
- *White lightweight paper*
- *Colored paper (We used Pacon® card stock, 8½" x 11," pastel)*
- *Black Tombow® Dual Brush Pen*

- *Glue stick*
- *Scissors*
- *Craft knife*
- *Cutting mat or magazine*
- *Ruler*
- *A7 envelope (we used a brown kraft mailer)*

OPTIONAL SUPPLIES*

- *Highlighters*
- *Neon circle stickers*
- *Tar rubber stamp*
- *Neon stamp pad*
- *Washi tape*

This is what we used, but have fun here—any stickers, markers, washi tape, rubber stamps, or other decorative flair will do!

I ♥ YOU CUZ...

FUNNY FACES

NINJA SKILLS

PILLOW FIGHTS !!!!!!!!!

SLOTH IMPRESSION

DANCE MOVES!

 YOUR CAT felix

PEANUT BUTTER COOKIES

HIGH FIVES

your infectious LAUGH

ALL the THINGS ♥♥♥

yas Queen

allison is AWESOME!

ALLISON LEE
40 CARL ST
SAN FRA...

CARD

1 Make your card. Cut the large sheet of lightweight paper down to 10" x 14," and fold it in half (to 10" x 7").

2 Make the portrait! With a pair of scissors, cut a head shape and body shape out of two colors of paper. Glue these to the inside of the card, on the right.

3 Cut two eye shapes from white paper, and glue on to the head. Using the Tombow® pen, draw the face, hair, and any other details. Use the Tombow® pen and highlighter to write a message.

4 Make the list! Cut two long strips of white paper. Using the Tombow® pen, write a list of things you love about the person you are sending the card to. Use a variety of type styles, and add funny doodles! Make sure to leave about ¾ inch blank at the bottom of the first strip to give yourself room to glue the two pieces together.

5 Place the second strip at a 90-degree angle to the first strip, and glue together using a glue stick. Add a bit of washi tape along the seam for flair.

6 Glue the list into the left side of the card (just a bit of glue along the top edge will do), and reinforce the top with washi tape.

7 Decorate the card with markers, washi tape, stickers, and rubber stamps.

8 Fold the list up so that it fits into the card, close the card, and then fold it in half horizontally so it fits into the envelope.

ENVELOPE

1 Using highlighters and washi tape, decorate the envelope to match.

IDEAS TO TRY

- List the places you want to travel to together

- List things you want to do together

GOOD EGG
Birthday CARD

Time to celebrate! This birthday card is egg-cellent for ALL ages.

MATERIALS

- 8½" x 11" sheet of white multimedia or hot-press watercolor paper
- 2.0 mm Molotow® Grafx Art Masking Liquid Pump Marker
- Neon acrylic or tempera paint
- Container for water
- Plate or palette

- Small pointed tip brush, size 2
- ½" or ¾" flat brush
- Black Tombow® Dual Brush Pen
- White, pink or red, and yellow Gelly Roll® pens
- Fine black felt-tip pen

- Pencil (optional)
- Eraser (optional)
- Craft knife
- Cutting mat or magazine
- Ruler
- A7 white envelope

48

CARD

1 Make your card. Fold a piece of multi-media or hot-press watercolor paper in half, and using a craft knife, ruler, and cutting mat or magazine, cut the card down to 5" x 7," folded.

2 Using the Molotow® marker, write the message, and draw six egg shapes (only the top $2/3$). Allow to dry for 5 to 10 minutes.

3 With acrylic or tempera, paint over the entire front of the card, going first from top to bottom, and then from side to side. Allow to dry, and then add another layer of paint. Continue to add layers of paint until you are happy with the saturation of color.

4 When the paint is almost dry, put the card under a stack of heavy books to make sure it dries flat.

5 When the card is completely dry, remove the masking fluid with your finger or an eraser.

6 With the fine tip of the Tombow® pen, add egg cups, faces, party hats and other details.

7 Add white details such as polka dots, stripes, and pom poms on the hats with a white gel or black fine tip paint pen.

8 Add cheeks with a pink or red neon Gelly Roll® pen.

PRO TIP

Rub the masking fluid off faster and cleaner with a fresh white eraser.

INSIDE GREETING IDEAS

● I hope you have an egg-cellent one!

● You crack me up.

50

ENVELOPE

1 Paint a pattern of vertical dashes in rows across the inside of the envelope flap, cutting off the pattern along the glue line of the envelope to create the illusion of an envelope liner. Let dry.

2 Draw flames with a yellow Gelly Roll® pen or a highlighter. Add black stripes and candlewicks.

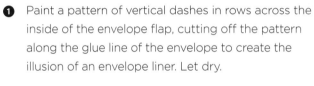

WILDLY GRATEFUL THANK YOU CARD

Gratitude just keeps giving! Just saying thank you feels great—and hearing it makes you feel special! Go wild and share love whenever you spot a reason to be grateful!

MATERIALS

- *8½" x 11" sheet of white card stock*
- *Watercolor paints*
- *Paintbrush*
- *Container for water*
- *Black Tombow® Dual Brush Pen*

- *Pencil*
- *Craft knife*
- *Cutting mat or magazine*
- *Ruler*
- *A7 white envelope*

IDEAS TO TRY

- You're the beary best! (Bear)
- Tank you! (Aquarium)
- Thanks a ton! (Elephant)
- You slay! (Tiger)

ALL HEART EYES ON YOU, GIRL.

CARD

1. Make your card. Fold a piece of white card stock in half, and using a craft knife, ruler, and cutting mat or magazine, cut the card to 5" x 7," folded.

2. With your brush and watercolors, paint the body of the leopard, the sun, and a few scattered asterisk shapes.

3. Using a pencil, lightly write out the message. When you are happy with the placement, go over the letters with the Tombow® pen, pressing harder on the downstroke to create this particular look.

4. Add the other black details using the brush tip for larger elements, such as the leaves and grass, and the finer point for the leopard spots and face.

ENVELOPE

1. Paint a matching pattern of leaves, grass, and other plants with watercolor, cutting off the pattern along the glue line of the envelope to create the illusion of an envelope liner.

SALTY Pretzel SORRY CARD

Sometimes we mess up, and that's OK—as long as we admit our shortcomings and make them right.
At the end of the day, nothing says "sorry" quite like a hand-crafted apology.
We like to add a dash of humor to keep it light. We'll laugh about this someday, right?

MATERIALS

- *8½" x 11" sheet of white card stock*
- *Neon pink tempera or acrylic paint*
- *Brush*
- *Plate or palette*
- *Black Tombow® Dual Brush Pen*
- *Pencil*

- *Eraser*
- *Tulip® Puffy™ Dimensional Fabric Paint*
- *Craft knife*
- *Cutting mat or magazine*
- *Ruler*
- *Highlighter*

IDEAS TO TRY

- Didn't mean to make you cry. (Onion)
- I blew it. (Candle)
- I suck. Sorry. (Lollipop)
- Sorry I was a little... (Poop emoji)
- Sorry I was crabby. (Crab)
- "My baaad." (Sheep)

CARD

1 Make your card. Fold a piece of card stock in half, and using a craft knife, ruler, and cutting mat or magazine, cut the card to 5" x 7," folded.

2 With a pencil, lightly trace the pretzel in the middle of the page. Then paint it with neon paint, and let it dry.

3 With a pencil, lightly write out the message. When you are happy with the placement, trace the message with the Tombow® Marker.

4 Using the Puffy™ paint, add dots of "salt" to the pretzel and let dry completely.

ENVELOPE

1 Grab your ruler and a highlighter. Place the envelope on a piece of scrap paper, and line the ruler parallel to the edge of your envelope and 1/4 inch away from the edge.

2 Holding your ruler, drag the highlighter along the edge of the card. Repeat for all envelope seams.

FRuiTY FRESH CARD

We love the fresh look of fruit slices for letting a friend know they're sweet. We used neon highlighters for pop and, for an unexpected twist, we paired the card with an envelope made from double-sided wrapping paper. Pick your favorite fruits, and let the fun begin!

MATERIALS

- *8½" x 11" sheet of white card stock*
- *Highlighters in red or pink, green, orange, and yellow*
- *¼ inch washi tape*
- *Black Tombow® Dual Brush Pen*
- *Scissors*

- *Pencil*
- *Eraser*
- *Fun wrapping paper for the envelope*

CARD

❶ Make your card. Cut out a circle from an 8.5" x 11" sheet of card stock, and fold it in half.

❷ Unfold the card, and place strips of washi tape to divide the circle into 8 sections. With an orange or green highlighter, trace the edge of the interior of the fruit, about ½ inch from the edge of the card, and color in the fruit.

❸ Carefully remove the washi tape. Using the flat edge of the highlighter, trace along the edge of the circle to create the outer edge of rind. With the yellow highlighter, trace a second line to fill in the rind.

❹ On the inside, write your message with a black Tombow® pen, and add fun drop shadows and details with the matching highlighter.

❺ For the watermelon, follow the same steps, skipping the washi tape. Instead of filling in the rind with yellow, leave that area white and draw black watermelon seeds with the small tip of the Tombow® marker.

ENVELOPE

❶ Make your own envelope (see directions on page 90) using a fun lightweight paper. We chose a double-sided wrapping paper from Meri Meri. Or you can use a plain envelope and doodle your own design on the inside flap.

INSIDE GREETING IDEAS

- I'd pick you any day.
- You make life so sweet.
- You're so sweet!
- Sweet on you!

YOU'RE SO FRESH!

SUNSHINE THANK YOU CARD

A happy sun is easy to doodle and will make someone's day. Start with a simple spot of yellow paint, then add doodles and hand-lettering. Try it with various styles and messages for different occasions!

MATERIALS

- *8½" x 11" sheet of white card stock*
- *Yellow tempera or acrylic paint*
- *Paintbrush*
- *Plate or palette*
- *Black crayon*

- *Pencil*
- *Craft knife*
- *Cutting mat or magazine*
- *Ruler*
- *A7 white envelope*

GREETING IDEAS

- You're my sunshine!
- You're so bright! Congrats, grad!
- Hello, sunshine!
- Stay golden!

CARD

1. Make your card. Fold a piece of card stock in half, and using a craft knife, ruler, and cutting mat or magazine, cut the card to 5" x 7," folded.

2. Paint a yellow circle and lines to make the sun and its rays. Let dry.

3. With a pencil, lightly write the message. Once you are happy with the placement, trace with a black crayon.

4. With the crayon, draw the face and dashed line detail on the rays.

ENVELOPE

1. Draw a grid pattern on the inside of the envelope with a black crayon, cutting off the pattern along the glue line of the envelope to create the illusion of an envelope liner.

PRO TIP

Paint the sun slightly higher on the page to give yourself room for the lettering.

65

YAY!!!!!!
Congrats CARD

This card is perfect for every occasion! Did someone do something extra nice for you? Did your friend's cat just have kittens? Pop a YAY!!!!!! Card in the mail!

MATERIALS

- *8½" x 11" sheet of multi-media or hot-press watercolor paper*
- *Pencil*
- *Eraser*
- *Watercolor paints*
- *Container for water*
- *Brush*

- *Black crayon*
- *Ruler*
- *Craft knife*
- *Cutting mat or magazine*
- *A7 white envelope*

CARD

1. Make your card. Fold a piece of multi-media or hot-press watercolor paper in half, and using a craft knife, ruler, and cutting mat or magazine, cut the card to 5" x 7," folded.

2. Using a pencil, draw the word "YAY" very lightly across the top half of the card. With a brush and watercolor paints, paint each letter. Let dry completely.

3. Using a black crayon, add smiley faces and exclamation points.

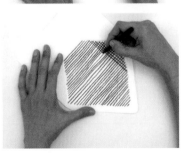

ENVELOPE

1. Draw a grid pattern on the inside of the envelope with a black crayon, cutting off the pattern along the glue line of the envelope to create the illusion of an envelope liner.

PRO TIP

If you are feeling uncertain about your hand-lettering skills, print out your message in a font you like, and trace onto your card using a tracing board or a window.

IDEAS TO TRY

- Thanks!!!
- Sorry!!!
- Yaaas!!!
- Oops!!!

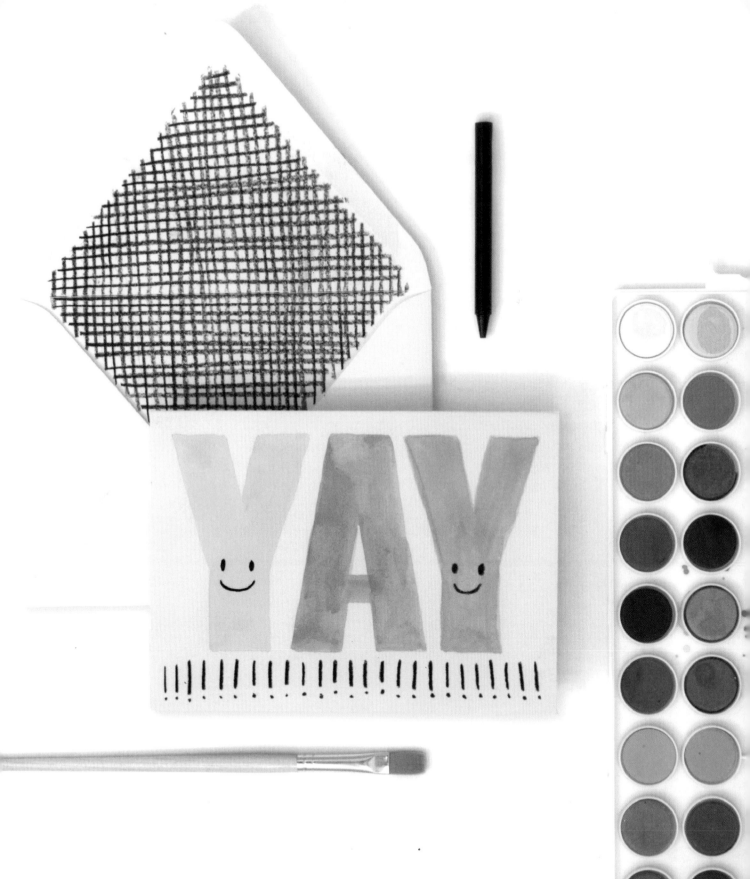

Random Holiday CARD

Every day is a holiday! There are tons of random holidays that you can celebrate.
We love finding funny, unexpected reasons to enjoy every day!

MATERIALS

- *8½" x 11" sheet of white card stock*
- *2 to 3 different colored rubber stamp pads*
- *3 pencils with eraser tops (optional for ice cream card)*
- *Erasers for carving*
- *¾-inch circle stickers (optional for umbrella card)*

- *Ruler*
- *Craft knife*
- *Cutting mat or magazine*
- *Black fine-tip pen*
- *A7 white envelope*

HOLIDAYS TO CONSIDER

- Peculiar People Day (January 10)
- Corn Dog Day (March 19)
- National Chicken Dance Day (May 14)
- National Ice Cream Day (July 17)

Even more ideas: http://www.
holidayscalendar.com/holidays/weird/

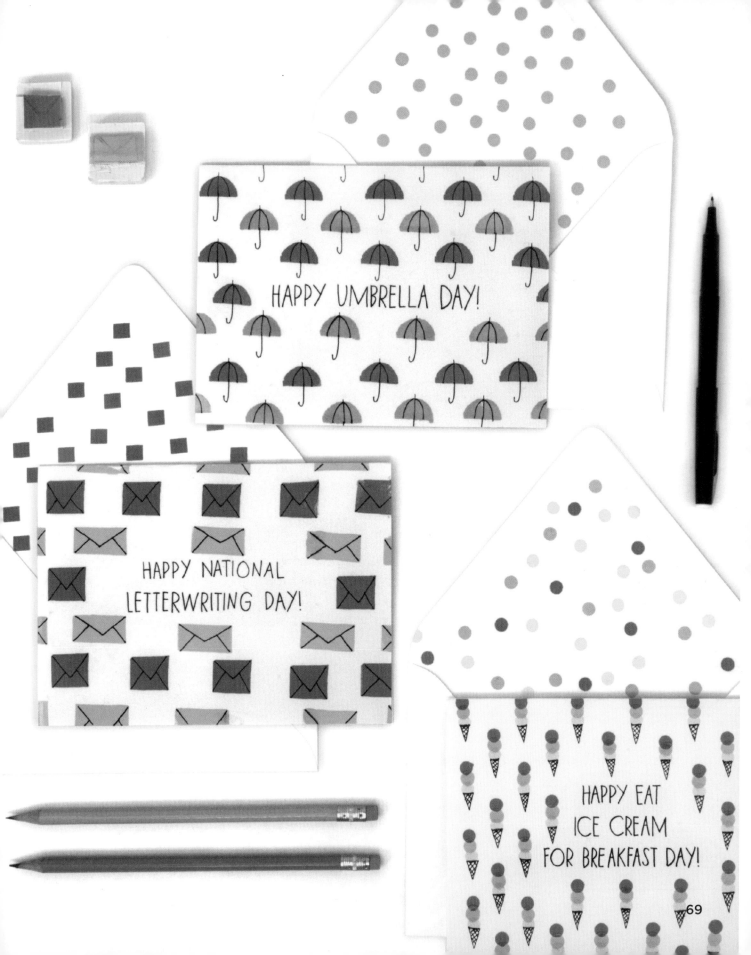

HAPPY UMBRELLA DAY!

HAPPY NATIONAL LETTERWRITING DAY!

HAPPY EAT ICE CREAM FOR BREAKFAST DAY!

CARD

1 Make your card. Fold a piece of card stock in half, and using a craft knife, ruler, and cutting mat or magazine, cut the card to 5" x 7," folded.

2 Write the message in the middle of the card with a fine black felt-tip pen.

3 Carve your stamp. Draw the shape you want to carve on the eraser with a pencil. (For our umbrella card, we used a $^3/_4$-inch circle sticker stuck to our eraser as a guide.) Once you are satisfied with your shape, use a craft knife to carve out any part of the eraser that is not part of the stamp to about $^1/_8$ inch deep. (For the ice cream card, we skipped this step. Instead, we used the eraser tops of three pencils as our stamps, one for each color.)

4 Stamp a pattern in alternating colors around the message. Make sure to leave space for additional details. Let dry.

5 Using a fine felt-tip marker, add additional details, such as ice cream cones, umbrella handles, envelope flaps, and so on.

PRO TIP

If you feel uncertain about your hand-lettering skills, print out your message in a font you like, and trace onto your card using a tracing board or a window.

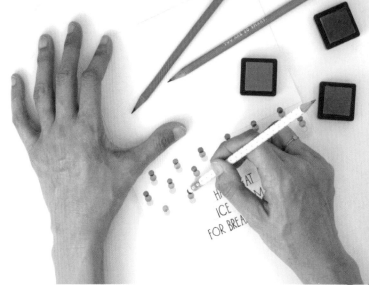

ENVELOPE

1 Using the eraser top of a pencil, stamp a pattern of dots on the envelope flap, cutting off the pattern along the glue line of the envelope to create the illusion of an envelope liner.

Pretty Personal Stationery

This is a necessity! You'll find there's always a time for pretty, simple stationery.
Here's a project that is dressed to impress and easy to execute.

MATERIALS

- *Several sheets of 8½" x 11" multi-media or hot-press watercolor paper*
- *Watercolors*
- *1 large and 1 fine brush*
- *Container for water*
- *White paint pen*

- *Black Tombow® Dual Brush Pen*
- *Craft knife*
- *Cutting mat or magazine*
- *Ruler*
- *A7 white envelope*

CARD

❶ Make your cards. Trim your paper to as many 5" x 7" flat rectangles as you want.

❷ With watercolors, paint various abstract circular shapes on each card.

❸ When the watercolor is almost dry, put the cards under a stack of heavy books to make sure they dry flat. Slip a sheet of scrap paper between each card so the color doesn't accidentally transfer from one card to another.

❹ When the cards are dry, add dashed line details with a small brush and watercolors. Add some white dashes with a paint pen for a little more depth. Let dry.

❺ With a Tombow® pen, write your name across the top of each card.

ENVELOPE

❶ With a small brush, paint a pattern of dashed lines on the inside flap of the envelope, cutting off the pattern along the glue line of the envelope to create the illusion of an envelope liner.

PRO TIP

A subtle design is best so it doesn't distract from your letter.

letter to your FUTURE SELF

Sometimes, you just want to freeze-frame a moment so that you remember the good times, life lessons, and epic experiences. In the future, you might be amazed at how far you've come!

MATERIALS

- *Rectangular sheet of white heavyweight paper (we used a 9" x 12" sheet of 90-lb. artist vellum)*
- *Small piece of white paper to make a label*
- *Highlighters in a variety of colors*
- *White paint pen*

- *Pencil*
- *Neon Gelly Roll® Pen*
- *Washi tape*
- *Scissors*
- *Ruler*

PRO TIP

Be sure to keep your letter in a safe place where you will be able to find it.

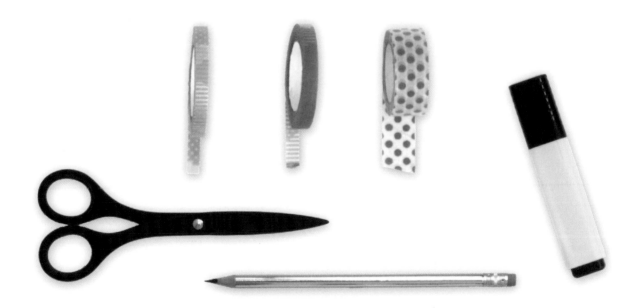

77

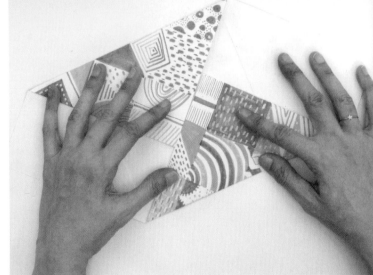

LETTER

❶ With a ruler and pencil, lightly draw a grid of 2-inch squares over the entire sheet of paper.

❷ Fill in each square with a different pattern, using two or three different colors of highlighter as the base, and then add details with the pencil and white paint pen.

❸ Write your letter on the other side in pencil.

ENVELOPE

❶ This letter turns into its own envelope. With the patterned side down, fold your letter widthwise in half, and then open your paper.

❷ Fold the bottom-right corner up and the upper-left corner down to meet the center fold and crease.

❸ Fold each side toward the middle, making sure they slightly overlap, and crease.

❹ Seal with a piece of washi tape.

❺ Cut out a rectangle from a sheet of white paper to make a label (sized so that it looks nice centered on the front of your folded-up and sealed letter). Cut off two opposite corners and, with a pencil, draw and write the details with dotted lines to fill in.

❻ Fill in the details with a neon Gelly Roll® pen.

Mother's Day / Father's Day Card

Nothing says "I love you" like a handmade card. For this project, we used one of our favorite tools, the Molotow® marker, to create an airy feel that's both polished and personal. Mom or Dad will love it!

MATERIALS

- *8½" x 11" sheet of multi-media or hot-press watercolor paper*
- *4.0 mm Molotow® Grafx Art Masking Liquid Pump Marker*
- *Watercolors*
- *Container for water*
- *Paintbrush*
- *Pencil (optional)*

- *Sakura Koi® Coloring Brush Pens or other markers in matching colors*
- *White eraser (optional)*
- *Craft knife*
- *Cutting mat or magazine*
- *Ruler*
- *A7 white envelope*

IDEAS TO TRY

- Love you, Mom (Floral doodles)
- Mom/Dad, I eat my vegetables! (Vegetable doodles)
- Love you, Dad (Tree doodles)
- Mom/Dad, you're my anchor (Anchor doodles)
- Dad, you've got it growin' on (Mustache doodles)

CARD

1 Make your card. Fold a piece of multi-media or hot-press watercolor paper in half, and using a craft knife, ruler, and cutting mat or magazine, cut the card to 5" x 7," folded.

2 Draw two horizontal parallel lines in the middle of your card with the Molotow® marker, and then write the message along the two lines. We encourage freehanding it, but you can always draw it first in pencil (draw very lightly so that you can erase the pencil afterward).

3 Doodle shapes around the message with the Molotow® marker. Allow to dry for 5 to 10 minutes.

4 Paint over the entire front of the card first with plain water, and then add watercolor paints. We used two shades of blue to achieve an ombre effect.

5 When the card is almost dry, put it under a stack of heavy books to make sure it dries flat.

6 When the card is completely dry, remove the masking fluid with your finger or an eraser.

PRO TIP

Rub the masking fluid off faster and cleaner with a fresh white eraser.

ENVELOPE

1 With similar-colored markers, doodle a matching pattern on the inside of the envelope, cutting off the pattern along the glue line of the envelope to create the illusion of an envelope liner.

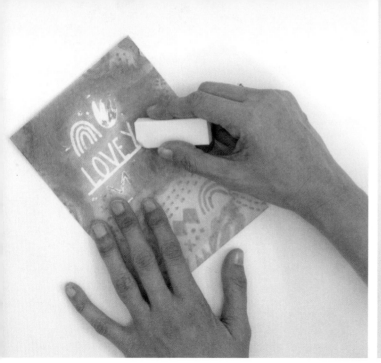

You're AWESOME SAUCE CARD

Sriracha®, Tapatío®, Tabasco®—they're all awesome! And so is the recipient of this card!
Let it be known with some handcrafted goodness.

MATERIALS

- 8½" x 11" sheet of multi-media or hot-press watercolor paper
- Neon tempera or acrylic paint
- Container for water
- Paintbrush
- Plate or palette
- Pencil
- Eraser
- White paint pen
- Black crayon
- Ruler
- Craft knife
- Cutting mat or magazine
- Newspaper to protect painting surface
- 3 sheets of scrap paper
- Washi or artist's tape
- A7 white envelope

CARD

1 Make your card. Fold a piece of multi-media or hot-press watercolor paper in half, and using a craft knife, ruler, and cutting mat or magazine, cut the card to 5" x 7," folded.

2 Paint a bottle shape in neon tempera or acrylic paint. Let dry completely.

3 With a pencil, lightly write out the message on the bottle. Once you are happy with the placement, trace over with a white paint pen. Let dry.

4 Using a black crayon, add the bottle top and lines.

INSIDE GREETING IDEAS

- Everything's better with you!
- You add a little spice to life.
- Stay spicy!

ENVELOPE

1 Place the envelope flap open, front side down on a piece of newspaper.

2 Place pieces of scrap paper along the inside edge the envelope opening, and tape off along the glue lines on the flap to keep them dry.

3 Mix paint with a bit of water. Load a brush with paint mixture, and flick it from above onto the envelope to create a splatter pattern.

Matisse-INSPIRED Selfie CARD

Be your colorful self! Embrace wacky colors and mixed media to make your selfie pop!

MATERIALS

- *8½" x 11" sheet of multi-media or hot-press watercolor paper*
- *Photo portrait sized to fit on a 5" x 7" card*
- *3 or 4 colors of tempera or acrylic paints*

- *White paper*
- *White Gelly Roll® pen*
- *Scissors*
- *Brush*
- *Container for water*
- *Plate or palette*

- *Glue stick*
- *Craft knife*
- *Cutting mat or magazine*
- *Ruler*
- *A7 white envelope*

CARD

1 Make your card. Fold a piece of multi-media or hot-press watercolor paper in half, and using a craft knife, ruler, and cutting mat or magazine, cut the card to 5" x 7," folded.

2 Cut around the photo to get rid of any background, and glue it to the front of the card.

3 Paint various abstract shapes around and over the photo. Let dry.

4 With a white Gelly Roll® pen, add some fun details, such as patterns of dashed lines and asterisks.

5 Add cut paper flourishes, such as diamonds, for additional depth.

LOOK UP, MATISSE'S CUT-OUTS ONLINE FOR SOME INSPIRATION!

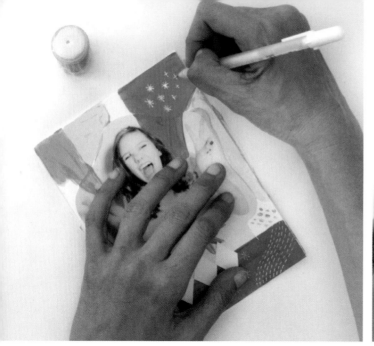

ENVELOPE

❶ Paint a pattern of various abstract shapes. Let dry.

❷ Add additional, finer details with a white Gelly Roll® pen.

GOOD VIBES ONLY

MAKE YOUR OWN ENVELOPE

Making your own envelopes is easy! Follow these steps to make a pro-looking envelope from scratch. It's a bit persnickety, but the end result is worth it!

- *Large piece of paper that's about 4 times the size of your card (for a 5"x 7" card, use a sheet of 11" x 17" paper)*
- *Ruler*

- *Pencil*
- *Scissors or craft knife*
- *Glue stick*

❶ Center your card diagonally on your piece of paper. Loosely trace a line around your card (add about ¼ inch to each side to give it room to slide out of the envelope easily). Remove your card, and mark the center of the rectangle with an X.

❷ Measure the distance from the X to point A (see image below). Now, measure that length plus ¾ inch from point A to point B; mark point B.

❸ Draw two lines from point B to the top corners of your rectangle to make the top flap (points C and D).

❹ Repeat steps 2 and 3 for the bottom and side flaps, this time only adding ¼ inch.

❺ Cut out the envelope with a craft knife and ruler or scissors. Fold in all four flaps along the line you traced around your card.

❻ Unfold the flaps. Neatly apply glue where the bottom flap overlaps the side flaps. Fold the bottom flap over the side flaps and press down to seal.

PRO TIP

Skip steps 1–4 above by pulling apart an envelope that fits your card and tracing its shape onto a sheet of paper!

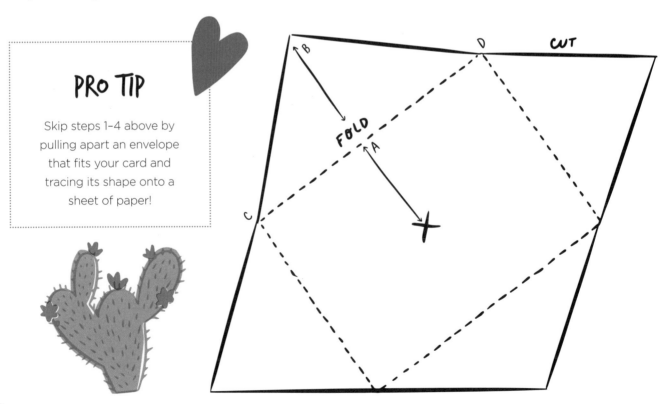

90

DRESS UP your ENVELOPE

Decorated envelopes will never get lost in the mail! Take a cue from the recipient's address (do they live near a beach? Draw a whale!), patterns that inspire you, or from something you wrote about in your letter!

MATERIALS

Get creative! In these examples, we used highlighters, Gelly Roll® pens, a pencil, Towbow® pens, and stickers. Just start doodling!

- **Whale envelope:** Draw a whale shape with a marker. Then add details with pencil and a neon red Gelly Roll® pen.

- **Cacti envelope:** Draw a variety of cactus shapes with a green highlighter. Add some flower and fruit shapes with a red highlighter.

- **Pretty feathers envelope:** Draw feathery shapes with a pale pink marker, and then add details and the recipient's address with a pencil.

Starry hand envelope: With a pencil, trace out the hand and the oval on the back flap, and write in the address and return address with a Tombow® pen. Use a black Sharpie® to color the entire envelope black, leaving the hand shape and oval white. Add the fingernails and any lines needed to define the fingers. Decorate the black areas with stars and dots with a white paint pen.

Cut paper envelope: Using neon and black paper, cut out letters and shapes, and glue them on with a glue stick. Write the address out with a Tombow® pen.

Sticker flowers envelope: These flowers are neon dot stickers with leaves and stems drawn with a Towbow® pen. Draw the stem and then add the sticker on top, working your way across the entire envelope.

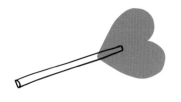

Stationery

HOW TO USE THIS SECTION

In this section, we've provided some designed cards and stationery for you to color in, write on, and decorate. Get inspired by what you've learned in this book to turn these pages into your own awesome hand-written cards and letters! If you want to mail the folded cards, get some A2 (4¼" x 5½") envelopes (or design your own!). The stationery sheets are self-mailing—just seal with a sticker before sending! Have fun!

Use these templates for the Emoji Note Cards on page 38.

Date ....

Dear .... ,

....

....

....

....

....

....

....

....

....

....

....

....

....

From: _____
‾‾‾‾‾‾‾‾‾‾‾‾‾‾‾‾
‾‾‾‾‾‾‾‾‾‾‾‾‾‾‾‾
‾‾‾‾‾‾‾‾‾‾‾‾‾‾‾‾

PLACE STAMP HERE

TO: _____
‾‾‾‾‾‾‾‾‾‾‾‾‾‾‾‾
‾‾‾‾‾‾‾‾‾‾‾‾‾‾‾‾
‾‾‾‾‾‾‾‾‾‾‾‾‾‾‾‾

DATE ....

DEAR ....

FROM

....

....

....

PLACE
STAMP
HERE

TO ....

....

....

DATE ....

DEAR ....

....

....

....

....

....

....

....

....

....

....

From:

SEND TO:

PLACE STAMP HERE ♥

From: _____

To: _____

Date _____

Dear _____

_____

_____

_____

_____

_____

_____

_____

_____

_____

_____

DATE ....

DEAR ....

....

....

....

....

....

....

....

....

....

....

FROM

....
....
....

TO

....
....
....

PLACE
STAMP
HERE

you do you.

HAPPY BIRTHDAY!
HOPE IT'S MAGICAL!

HAVE A SUPER SWEET BIRTHDAY!

....

....

....

....

....

....

....

....

....

....

....

....

....

....

....

....

....

....

....

....

THANKS A BUNCH!

HAPPY BIRTHDAY!

YOU ARE SO EGG-CELLENT!

SEE YA LATER ALLIGATOR!

0000

HAPPY BIRTHDAY!

HAVE A WHALE OF A BIRTHDAY!

dive in!

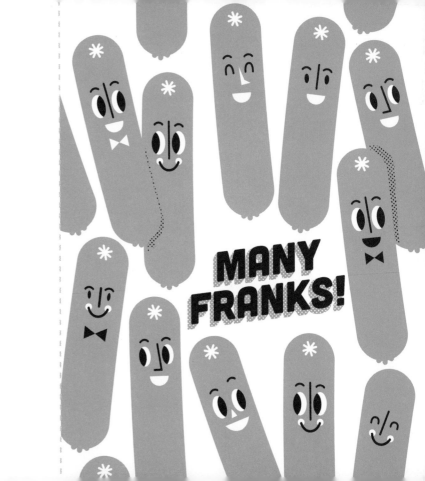

....

....

....

....

....

....

....

....

....

....

....

GO NUTS!

HAVE A SWEET BIRTHDAY!

WILDLY GRATEFUL

....

....

....

....

....

....

....

....

....

....

12

....

....

....

....

....

....

....

....

....

....

....

SO GLAD

WE'RE TIGHT!

HAVE A **PURR-FECT** Birthday!

....
....
....
....
....
....
....
....
....
....
....

....
....
....
....
....
....
....
....
....
....
....